A Trip to the
LIBRARY
with SESAME STREET

Christy Peterson

Lerner Publications ◆ Minneapolis
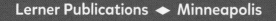

Elmo and his friends from *Sesame Street* are going on a field trip, and you're invited! Field trips provide children with the opportunity to explore their communities, visit new places, and experience hands-on learning. This series brings the joys of field trips to your fingertips. Where will you go next?

—Sincerely, the Editors at Sesame Street

TABLE OF CONTENTS

LET'S VISIT THE LIBRARY!

A library is an important part of a community. You can go there to borrow books, use computers, and more. Today we get to see how a library works.

Elmo loves to read with his friends!

A library has many books. Each book has its own number. Library workers put the books on the shelves in order by number.

There are so many books! Let's count them. One, two, three . . .

There are too many! We will miss the tour.

People use the computers to find a book's number. They also use computers to play games or look up information.

I like to use the computers to learn more about music from all over the world!

A librarian helps people check out books. The librarian also lets them know when to bring the books back.

I'm careful not to get any oatmeal on my book so it's clean for the next person.

I keep my book in a special place so I remember to bring it back.

This person is returning their books to a return bin outside of the library. The books slide through a slot and into a bin so they can be put back on the shelf for the next person.

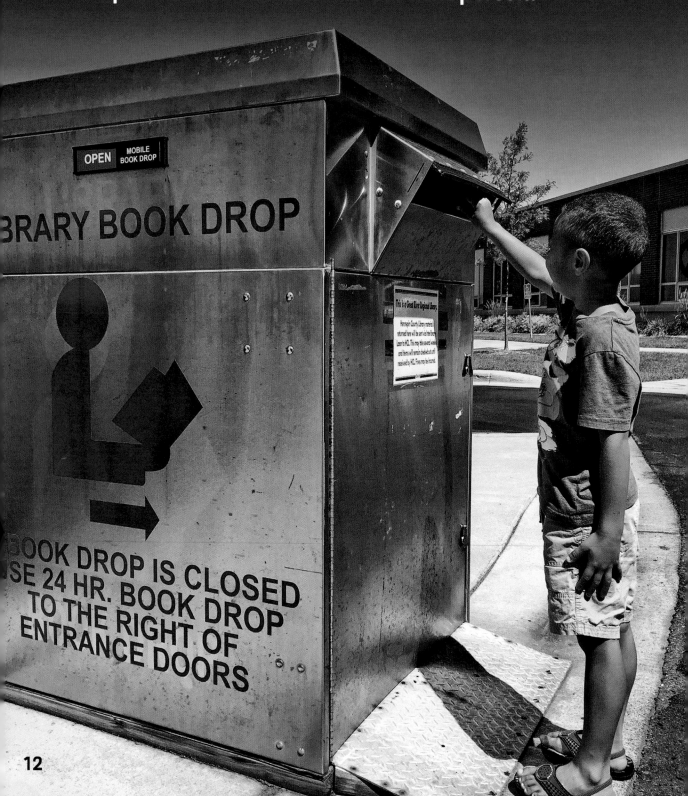

OPEN MOBILE BOOK DROP

BRARY BOOK DROP

BOOK DROP IS CLOSED
SE 24 HR. BOOK DROP
TO THE RIGHT OF
ENTRANCE DOORS

Some people come to libraries to read, study, or work. We show respect to them by using indoor voices.

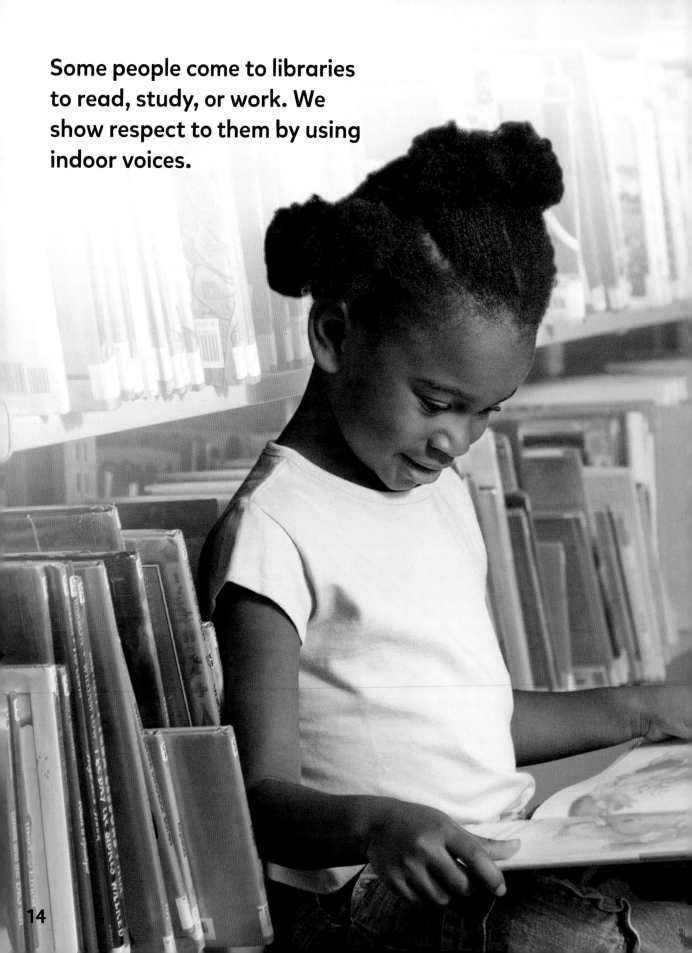

Libraries have more than books. People can check out movies and music too.

At my library, you can check out board games.

There is a lot going on at the library. There are language classes, story time, and clubs to join.

Me found a cookie cookbook!

Today we get to check out a book. What books do you like to find at your library?

THE LIBRARY AT HOME

You can check out books too. Ask a grown-up to take you to the library. If you don't have a library card, ask a librarian. You will be given a form to fill out. An adult can help you fill it out. You'll get to write your name on your card. Now you can check out books!

GLOSSARY

community: a group of people who live in the same area

computer: a machine that helps organize and retrieve data

language: words or signs that people use to talk to one another

librarian: a person who has special training to work with books and other materials

LEARN MORE

Ardely, Anthony. *I Can Be a Librarian.* New York: Gareth Stevens, 2019.

Clark, Rosalyn. *A Visit to the Library.* Minneapolis: Lerner Publications, 2018.

Kawa, Katie. *A Day with a Librarian.* New York: Cavendish Square, 2021.

INDEX

PHOTO ACKNOWLEDGMENTS

Image credits: Independent Picture Service, pp. 4, 7; wavebreakmedia/Shutterstock.com, p. 6; Rob Marmion/Shutterstock.com, p. 8; Tyler Olson/Shutterstock.com, p. 10; iliveoak/Stockimo/Alamy Stock Photo, p. 12; Dave & Les Jacobs/DigitalVision/Getty Images, p. 14; Randy Duchaine/Alamy Stock Photo, p. 16; Westend61/Getty Images, p. 17; ESB Professional/Shutterstock.com, p. 18; Klaus Vedfelt/DigitalVision/Getty Images, p. 20.

Cover: Andersen Ross Photography Inc/DigitalVision/Getty Images.

Lerner Publications Company
An imprint of Lerner Publishing Group, Inc.
241 First Avenue North
Minneapolis, MN 55401 USA

For reading levels and more information, look up this title at www.lernerbooks.com.

Main body text set in Mikado a.
Typeface provided by HVD Fonts.

Editor: Rebecca Higgins
Lerner team: Sue Marquis

Library of Congress Cataloging-in-Publication Data

Names: Peterson, Christy, author.
Title: A trip to the library with Sesame Street / Christy Peterson.
Description: Minneapolis : Lerner Publications, [2022] | Series: Sesame Street field trips | Includes bibliographical references and index. | Audience: Ages 4–8. | Audience: Grades K–1. | Summary: "The Sesame Street gang goes to the library and invites readers along to discover how libraries play an important role in communities. Readers learn how to sign up for their own library cards too!"– Provided by publisher.
Identifiers: LCCN 2021010415 (print) | LCCN 2021010416 (ebook) | ISBN 9781728439167 (library binding) | ISBN 9781728445076 (ebook)
Subjects: LCSH: Libraries—Juvenile literature.
Classification: LCC Z665.5 .P48 2022 (print) | LCC Z665.5 (ebook) | DDC 027—dc23

LC record available at https://lccn.loc.gov/2021010415
LC ebook record available at https://lccn.loc.gov/2021010416

Manufactured in the United States of America
1-49822-49690-9/1/2021